The Post Office

Julie Murray

Abdo

MY COMMUNITY: PLACES

Kids

abdopublishing.com

Published by Abdo Kids, a division of ABDO, PO Box 398166, Minneapolis, Minnesota 55439.
Copyright © 2017 by Abdo Consulting Group, Inc. International copyrights reserved in all countries.
No part of this book may be reproduced in any form without written permission from the publisher.

Printed in the United States of America, North Mankato, Minnesota.

052016

092016

Photo Credits: Alamy, AP Images, iStock, Shutterstock, ©Supannee Hickman p.22 / Shutterstock.com

Production Contributors: Teddy Borth, Jennie Forsberg, Grace Hansen

Design Contributors: Christina Doffing, Candice Keimig, Dorothy Toth

Cataloging-in-Publication Data

Names: Murray, Julie, author.

Title: The post office / by Julie Murray.

Description: Minneapolis, MN : Abdo Kids, [2017] | Series: My community: places
    | Includes bibliographical references and index.

Identifiers: LCCN 2015959211 | ISBN 9781680805390 (lib. bdg.) |
    ISBN 9781680805956 (ebook) | ISBN 9781680806519 (Read-to-me ebook)

Subjects: LCSH: Postal service--Juvenile literature. | Buildings--Juvenile literature.

Classification: DDC 383--dc23

LC record available at http://lccn.loc.gov/2015959211

Table of Contents

The Post Office

The post office is a special place. All the mail comes here. That is a lot of mail!

Ian works here. He is a

postal worker.

Kayla goes to the post office.

She mails a letter.

Nora buys a stamp.

She puts it on her letter.

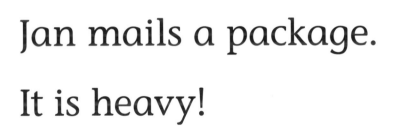

Jan mails a package.

It is heavy!

All the mail gets a **postmark**.

It shows the date it was mailed.

The mail is **sorted**.

Amy sorts the mail.

17

The mail is put on trucks.

Mike delivers the mail.

UNITED STATES POSTAL SERVICE

Have you been to a post office?

MAIL DROP

LETTERS

Stamps & Other Servic

Stamps
Money Orders
Passports
Passport Photos
PO Boxes

United States
Post Office®

↑ Mail Drop

↖ Self Service

← Window Service
U.S. & International Shipping
Money Orders
Insurance
Delivery Confirmation™
Service
International Wire Transfers
Stamps

→ The Postal Store®

Priority Mail Flat Rate Boxes
A simpler way to ship.

At the Post Office

letter

package

mail truck

stamp

Glossary

postmark
an official mark stamped on letters and mail.

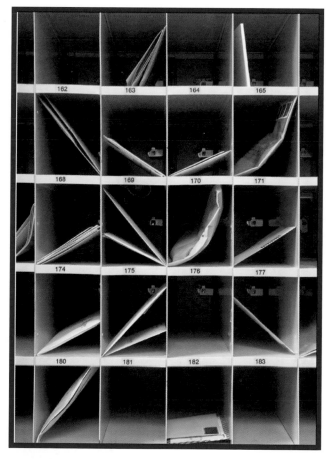

sort
to separate and put in a certain order.

Index

abdokids.com

Use this code to log on to abdokids.com and access crafts, games, videos, and more!

Abdo Kids Code:

MTK5390